Plot your way to success...

I hope you enjoy this Allotment Planner.
I created this after being frustrated when searching through my huge box of seed packets every time I couldn't remember something about a particular plant. I wanted somewhere to record when it could be sown, how far it needed to be spaced, when to plant out etc. Plus I wanted to design my plot. I couldn't find a planner with everything I wanted in it so I decided to design my own.

I am a small business and I would be grateful if you could leave a review as it helps my books to be seen so that others can buy them too, thanks in advance!

MY PLOT / GARDEN INFORMATION

SOIL TYPE:
_____

PH:
_____

LAST FROST DATE (SPRING)
_____

FIRST FROST DATE (AUTUMN)
_____

SUN LOCATION:

Morning: _____

Midday: _____

Afternoon: _____

AREAS OF WIND EXPOSURE:
_____

TOTAL GROWING AREA:
_____

PLANTS I WOULD LIKE TO GROW:

_____	_____
_____	_____
_____	_____
_____	_____
_____	_____
_____	_____
_____	_____
_____	_____
_____	_____

OTHER NOTES:
_____
_____
_____
_____
_____

MY PLOT LAYOUT

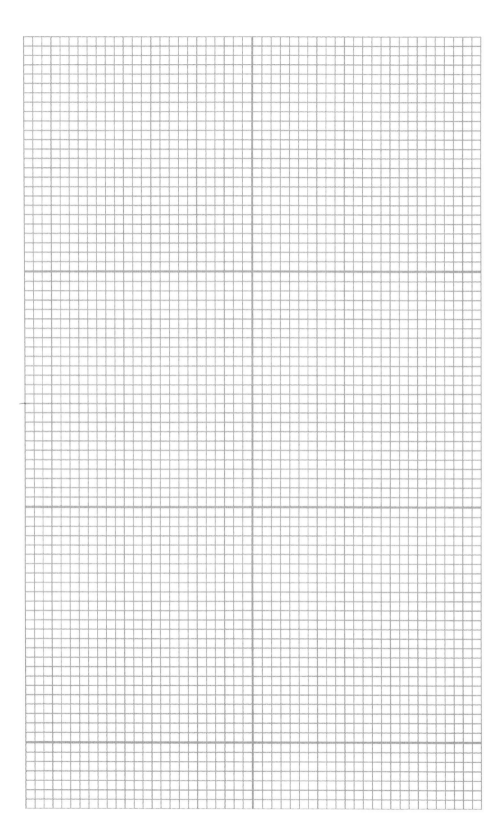

MY PLOT LAYOUT
Crop Rotation / Next Season

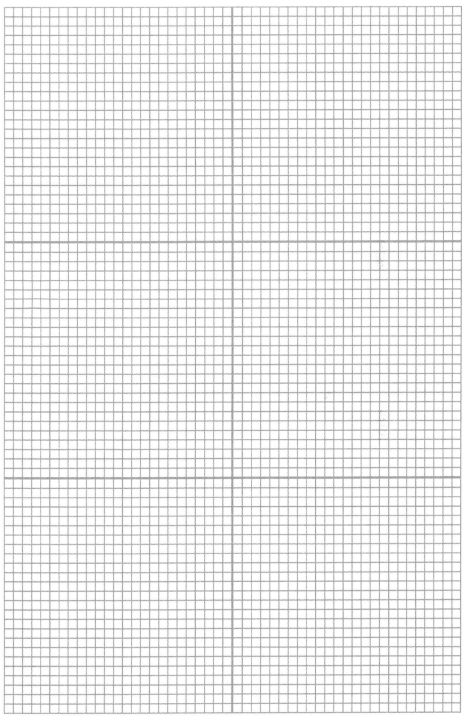

ALLOTMENT WISH LIST

ALLOTMENT PROJECTS

DETAILS: DONE:

- _____ ☐ Date:
- _____ ☐ Date:
- _____ ☐ Date:
- _____ ☐ Date:
- _____ ☐ Date:
- _____ ☐ Date:
- _____ ☐ Date:
- _____ ☐ Date:
- _____ ☐ Date:
- _____ ☐ Date:
- _____ ☐ Date:
- _____ ☐ Date:

ALLOTMENT PROJECTS

DETAILS: **DONE:**

Details	Done	Date
	☐	
	☐	
	☐	
	☐	
	☐	
	☐	
	☐	
	☐	
	☐	
	☐	
	☐	
	☐	

SEED INVENTORY

CROP	VARIETY	SEED CO.	PACK SIZE	YEAR	EXP	QTY LEFT	ORDER MORE?

SEED INVENTORY

CROP	VARIETY	SEED CO.	PACK SIZE	YEAR	EXP	QTY LEFT	ORDER MORE?

SEED INVENTORY

CROP	VARIETY	SEED CO.	PACK SIZE	YEAR	EXP	QTY LEFT	ORDER MORE?

SEED INVENTORY

CROP	VARIETY	SEED CO.	PACK SIZE	YEAR	EXP	QTY LEFT	ORDER MORE?

SEED INVENTORY

CROP	VARIETY	SEED CO.	PACK SIZE	YEAR	EXP	QTY LEFT	ORDER MORE?

BULB INVENTORY

CROP	VARIETY	SEED CO.	PACK SIZE	YEAR	EXP	QTY LEFT	ORDER MORE?

SEEDS TO BUY OR TRY

CROP	VARIETY	SEED CO.	NOTES

SEEDS TO BUY OR TRY

CROP	VARIETY	SEED CO.	NOTES

SEEDS TO BUY OR TRY

CROP	VARIETY	SEED CO.	NOTES

SEEDS TO BUY OR TRY

CROP	VARIETY	SEED CO.	NOTES

SEED SOWING LIST

CROP	VARIETY	SEED CO.	DATE SOWN	SEEDLINGS APPEAR	POTTED ON

SEED SOWING LIST

CROP	VARIETY	SEED CO.	DATE SOWN	SEEDLINGS APPEAR	POTTED ON

SEED SOWING LIST

CROP	VARIETY	SEED CO.	DATE SOWN	SEEDLINGS APPEAR	POTTED ON

SEED SOWING LIST

CROP	VARIETY	SEED CO.	DATE SOWN	SEEDLINGS APPEAR	POTTED ON

SEED SOWING LIST

CROP	VARIETY	SEED CO.	DATE SOWN	SEEDLINGS APPEAR	POTTED ON

SEED SOWING LIST

CROP	VARIETY	SEED CO.	DATE SOWN	SEEDLINGS APPEAR	POTTED ON

PLANTING OUT LOG

CROP	VARIETY	DATE	LOCATION

PLANTING OUT LOG

CROP	VARIETY	DATE	LOCATION

PLANTING OUT LOG

CROP	VARIETY	DATE	LOCATION

PLANTING OUT LOG

CROP	VARIETY	DATE	LOCATION

PLANTING OUT LOG

CROP	VARIETY	DATE	LOCATION

PLANTING OUT LOG

CROP	VARIETY	DATE	LOCATION

HARVEST LOG

CROP & VARIETY	FIRST HARVEST	LAST HARVEST	COMMENTS

HARVEST LOG

CROP & VARIETY	FIRST HARVEST	LAST HARVEST	COMMENTS

HARVEST LOG

CROP & VARIETY	FIRST HARVEST	LAST HARVEST	COMMENTS

HARVEST LOG

CROP & VARIETY	FIRST HARVEST	LAST HARVEST	COMMENTS

BLOOM LOG - SPRING/SUMMER

FLOWER: DATE:

BLOOM LOG - FALL/WINTER

FLOWER: DATE:

SEED SAVING LOG

CROP	VARIETY	DATE	COMMENTS

SEED SAVING LOG

CROP	VARIETY	DATE	COMMENTS

PESTS AND DISEASES

PEST/DISEASE:	PREVENTION / TREATMENT:	RESULTS:

PESTS AND DISEASES

PEST/DISEASE: **PREVENTION / TREATMENT:** **RESULTS:**

THINGS TO DO IN JANUARY

JANUARY NOTES

THINGS TO DO IN FEBRUARY

FEBRUARY NOTES

THINGS TO DO IN MARCH

THINGS TO DO IN MARCH

MARCH NOTES

MARCH NOTES

THINGS TO DO IN APRIL

THINGS TO DO IN APRIL

APRIL NOTES

 # APRIL NOTES

THINGS TO DO IN MAY

THINGS TO DO IN MAY

MAY NOTES

MAY NOTES

THINGS TO DO IN JUNE

THINGS TO DO IN JUNE

JUNE NOTES

JUNE NOTES

THINGS TO DO IN JULY

THINGS TO DO IN JULY

JULY NOTES

 # JULY NOTES

THINGS TO DO IN AUGUST

THINGS TO DO IN AUGUST

AUGUST NOTES

 # AUGUST NOTES

THINGS TO DO IN SEPTEMBER

THINGS TO DO IN SEPTEMBER

SEPTEMBER NOTES

SEPTEMBER NOTES

THINGS TO DO IN OCTOBER

THINGS TO DO IN OCTOBER

OCTOBER NOTES

OCTOBER NOTES

THINGS TO DO IN NOVEMBER

NOVEMBER NOTES

THINGS TO DO IN DECEMBER

DECEMBER NOTES

PLANT INFORMATION SHEET

PLANT NAME: _____   VARIETY: _____

TYPE: Seed / Cutting / Plug Plant / Bulb

LIFE CYCLE: Annual / Biennial / Perennial

GOOD COMPANION FOR:
_____
_____
_____

BAD COMPANION FOR:
_____
_____
_____

	J	F	M	A	M	J	J	A	S	O	N	D
SOW:												
PLANT OUT:												
HARVEST/BLOOM:												

SOWING METHOD: Indoors / Direct / Seed bed

FINAL GROWING LOCATION: Outdoors / Polytunnel / Greenhouse

PLANT SPACING: _____

SOIL TYPE: _____

SUN: All day / Partial / Shade

ATTRACTOR FOR: _____
_____

REPELLENT TO: _____
_____

CROP ROTATION FREQUENCY:
_____

NEEDS SUPPORT: Yes / No

FEED WITH: _____
Frequency: _____

SOW IN SUCCESSION: Yes / No
Frequency: _____

MULCH: Yes/No   MANURE: Yes/No
Type: _____   Type: _____

WATER FREQUENCY:
_____

FROST TOLERANCE: Yes / No

PEST ISSUES: _____   SOLUTIONS: _____
_____   _____
_____   _____

OTHER THINGS TO NOTE: _____
_____

PLANT INFORMATION SHEET

PLANT NAME: _____

VARIETY: _____

TYPE:
Seed / Cutting / Plug Plant / Bulb

LIFE CYCLE:
Annual / Biennial / Perennial

GOOD COMPANION FOR:
_____
_____
_____

BAD COMPANION FOR:
_____
_____
_____

	J	F	M	A	M	J	J	A	S	O	N	D
SOW:												
PLANT OUT:												
HARVEST/BLOOM:												

SOWING METHOD:
Indoors / Direct / Seed bed

FINAL GROWING LOCATION:
Outdoors / Polytunnel / Greenhouse

PLANT SPACING: _____

SOIL TYPE: _____

SUN: All day / Partial / Shade

ATTRACTOR FOR: _____
_____

REPELLENT TO: _____
_____

CROP ROTATION FREQUENCY:
_____

NEEDS SUPPORT: Yes / No

FEED WITH: _____
Frequency: _____

SOW IN SUCCESSION: Yes / No
Frequency. _____

MULCH: Yes/No   MANURE: Yes/No
Type: _____   Type: _____

WATER FREQUENCY:
_____

FROST TOLERANCE: Yes / No

PEST ISSUES: SOLUTIONS:
_____   _____
_____   _____

OTHER THINGS TO NOTE: _____
_____

PLANT INFORMATION SHEET

PLANT NAME: _____

VARIETY: _____

TYPE:
Seed / Cutting / Plug Plant / Bulb

LIFE CYCLE:
Annual / Biennial / Perennial

GOOD COMPANION FOR:
_____
_____

BAD COMPANION FOR:
_____
_____

	J	F	M	A	M	J	J	A	S	O	N	D
SOW:												
PLANT OUT:												
HARVEST/BLOOM:												

SOWING METHOD:
Indoors / Direct / Seed bed

FINAL GROWING LOCATION:
Outdoors / Polytunnel / Greenhouse

PLANT SPACING: _____

SOIL TYPE: _____

SUN: All day / Partial / Shade

ATTRACTOR FOR: _____
_____

REPELLENT TO: _____
_____

CROP ROTATION FREQUENCY:
_____

NEEDS SUPPORT: Yes / No

FEED WITH: _____
Frequency: _____

SOW IN SUCCESSION: Yes / No
Frequency: _____

MULCH: Yes/No   MANURE: Yes/No
Type: _____   Type: _____

WATER FREQUENCY:
_____

FROST TOLERANCE: Yes / No

PEST ISSUES: SOLUTIONS:
_____   _____
_____   _____
_____   _____

OTHER THINGS TO NOTE: _____
_____

PLANT INFORMATION SHEET

PLANT NAME: _____

VARIETY: _____

TYPE:
Seed / Cutting / Plug Plant / Bulb

LIFE CYCLE:
Annual / Biennial / Perennial

GOOD COMPANION FOR:
_____
_____
_____

BAD COMPANION FOR:
_____
_____
_____

	J	F	M	A	M	J	J	A	S	O	N	D
SOW:												
PLANT OUT:												
HARVEST/BLOOM:												

SOWING METHOD:
Indoors / Direct / Seed bed

FINAL GROWING LOCATION:
Outdoors / Polytunnel / Greenhouse

PLANT SPACING: _____

SOIL TYPE: _____

SUN: All day / Partial / Shade

ATTRACTOR FOR: _____
_____

REPELLENT TO: _____
_____

CROP ROTATION FREQUENCY:
_____

NEEDS SUPPORT: Yes / No

FEED WITH: _____
Frequency: _____

SOW IN SUCCESSION: Yes / No
Frequency: _____

MULCH: Yes/No   MANURE: Yes/No
Type: _____   Type: _____

WATER FREQUENCY:
_____

FROST TOLERANCE: Yes / No

PEST ISSUES: SOLUTIONS:
_____   _____
_____   _____
_____   _____

OTHER THINGS TO NOTE: _____
_____

PLANT INFORMATION SHEET

PLANT NAME: _____

VARIETY: _____

TYPE:
Seed / Cutting / Plug Plant / Bulb

LIFE CYCLE:
Annual / Biennial / Perennial

GOOD COMPANION FOR:
_____
_____
_____

BAD COMPANION FOR:
_____
_____
_____

	J	F	M	A	M	J	J	A	S	O	N	D
SOW:												
PLANT OUT:												
HARVEST/BLOOM:												

SOWING METHOD:
Indoors / Direct / Seed bed

NEEDS SUPPORT: Yes / No

FINAL GROWING LOCATION:
Outdoors / Polytunnel / Greenhouse

FEED WITH: _____
Frequency: _____

PLANT SPACING: _____

SOW IN SUCCESSION: Yes / No
Frequency: _____

SOIL TYPE: _____

MULCH: Yes/No   MANURE: Yes/No
Type: _____   Type: _____

SUN: All day / Partial / Shade

ATTRACTOR FOR: _____
_____

WATER FREQUENCY:
_____

REPELLENT TO: _____
_____

FROST TOLERANCE: Yes / No

PEST ISSUES: SOLUTIONS:
_____   _____
_____   _____
_____   _____

CROP ROTATION FREQUENCY:
_____

OTHER THINGS TO NOTE: _____
_____

PLANT INFORMATION SHEET

PLANT NAME: _____

VARIETY: _____

TYPE:
Seed / Cutting / Plug Plant / Bulb

LIFE CYCLE:
Annual / Biennial / Perennial

GOOD COMPANION FOR:
_____
_____
_____

BAD COMPANION FOR:
_____
_____
_____

	J	F	M	A	M	J	J	A	S	O	N	D
SOW:												
PLANT OUT:												
HARVEST/BLOOM:												

SOWING METHOD:
Indoors / Direct / Seed bed

FINAL GROWING LOCATION:
Outdoors / Polytunnel / Greenhouse

PLANT SPACING: _____

SOIL TYPE: _____

SUN: All day / Partial / Shade

ATTRACTOR FOR: _____
_____

REPELLENT TO: _____
_____

CROP ROTATION FREQUENCY:
_____

NEEDS SUPPORT: Yes / No

FEED WITH: _____
Frequency: _____

SOW IN SUCCESSION: Yes / No
Frequency: _____

MULCH: Yes/No   MANURE: Yes/No
Type: _____   Type: _____

WATER FREQUENCY:
_____

FROST TOLERANCE: Yes / No

PEST ISSUES: SOLUTIONS:
_____   _____
_____   _____
_____   _____

OTHER THINGS TO NOTE: _____
_____

PLANT INFORMATION SHEET

PLANT NAME: _____

VARIETY: _____

TYPE:
Seed / Cutting / Plug Plant / Bulb

LIFE CYCLE:
Annual / Biennial / Perennial

GOOD COMPANION FOR:
_____
_____
_____

BAD COMPANION FOR:
_____
_____
_____

	J	F	M	A	M	J	J	A	S	O	N	D
SOW:												
PLANT OUT:												
HARVEST/BLOOM:												

SOWING METHOD:
Indoors / Direct / Seed bed

FINAL GROWING LOCATION:
Outdoors / Polytunnel / Greenhouse

PLANT SPACING: _____

SOIL TYPE: _____

SUN: All day / Partial / Shade

ATTRACTOR FOR: _____
_____

REPELLENT TO: _____
_____

CROP ROTATION FREQUENCY:
_____

NEEDS SUPPORT: Yes / No

FEED WITH: _____
Frequency: _____

SOW IN SUCCESSION: Yes / No
Frequency: _____

MULCH: Yes/No   MANURE: Yes/No
Type: _____   Type: _____

WATER FREQUENCY:
_____

FROST TOLERANCE: Yes / No

PEST ISSUES: SOLUTIONS:
_____   _____
_____   _____
_____   _____

OTHER THINGS TO NOTE: _____
_____

PLANT INFORMATION SHEET

PLANT NAME: _____

VARIETY: _____

TYPE:
Seed / Cutting / Plug Plant / Bulb

LIFE CYCLE:
Annual / Biennial / Perennial

GOOD COMPANION FOR:
_____
_____

BAD COMPANION FOR:
_____
_____

	J	F	M	A	M	J	J	A	S	O	N	D
SOW:												
PLANT OUT:												
HARVEST/BLOOM:												

SOWING METHOD:
Indoors / Direct / Seed bed

NEEDS SUPPORT: Yes / No

FEED WITH: _____
Frequency: _____

FINAL GROWING LOCATION:
Outdoors / Polytunnel / Greenhouse

SOW IN SUCCESSION: Yes / No
Frequency: _____

PLANT SPACING: _____

SOIL TYPE: _____

MULCH: Yes/No   MANURE: Yes/No
Type: _____   Type: _____

SUN: All day / Partial / Shade

ATTRACTOR FOR: _____
_____

WATER FREQUENCY:
_____

REPELLENT TO: _____
_____

FROST TOLERANCE: Yes / No

PEST ISSUES: SOLUTIONS:
_____   _____
_____   _____

CROP ROTATION FREQUENCY:
_____

OTHER THINGS TO NOTE: _____
_____

PLANT INFORMATION SHEET

PLANT NAME: _____ VARIETY: _____

TYPE:
Seed / Cutting / Plug Plant / Bulb

LIFE CYCLE:
Annual / Biennial / Perennial

GOOD COMPANION FOR:
_____
_____
_____

BAD COMPANION FOR:
_____
_____
_____

	J	F	M	A	M	J	J	A	S	O	N	D
SOW:												
PLANT OUT:												
HARVEST/BLOOM:												

SOWING METHOD:
Indoors / Direct / Seed bed

FINAL GROWING LOCATION:
Outdoors / Polytunnel / Greenhouse

PLANT SPACING: _____

SOIL TYPE: _____

SUN: All day / Partial / Shade

ATTRACTOR FOR: _____
_____

REPELLENT TO: _____
_____

CROP ROTATION FREQUENCY:
_____

NEEDS SUPPORT: Yes / No

FEED WITH: _____
Frequency: _____

SOW IN SUCCESSION: Yes / No
Frequency: _____

MULCH: Yes/No   MANURE: Yes/No
Type: _____   Type: _____

WATER FREQUENCY:
_____

FROST TOLERANCE: Yes / No

PEST ISSUES: SOLUTIONS:
_____   _____
_____   _____
_____   _____

OTHER THINGS TO NOTE: _____
_____

PLANT INFORMATION SHEET

PLANT NAME: _____

VARIETY: _____

TYPE:
Seed / Cutting / Plug Plant / Bulb

LIFE CYCLE:
Annual / Biennial / Perennial

GOOD COMPANION FOR:
_____
_____
_____

BAD COMPANION FOR:
_____
_____
_____

	J	F	M	A	M	J	J	A	S	O	N	D
SOW:												
PLANT OUT:												
HARVEST/BLOOM:												

SOWING METHOD:
Indoors / Direct / Seed bed

FINAL GROWING LOCATION:
Outdoors / Polytunnel / Greenhouse

PLANT SPACING: _____

SOIL TYPE: _____

SUN: All day / Partial / Shade

ATTRACTOR FOR: _____
_____

REPELLENT TO: _____
_____

CROP ROTATION FREQUENCY:
_____

NEEDS SUPPORT: Yes / No

FEED WITH: _____
Frequency: _____

SOW IN SUCCESSION: Yes / No
Frequency: _____

MULCH: Yes/No   MANURE: Yes/No
Type: _____   Type: _____

WATER FREQUENCY:
_____

FROST TOLERANCE: Yes / No

PEST ISSUES: SOLUTIONS:
_____   _____
_____   _____
_____   _____

OTHER THINGS TO NOTE: _____
_____

PLANT INFORMATION SHEET

PLANT NAME: _____ VARIETY: _____

TYPE:
Seed / Cutting / Plug Plant / Bulb

LIFE CYCLE:
Annual / Biennial / Perennial

GOOD COMPANION FOR:
_____
_____
_____

BAD COMPANION FOR:
_____
_____
_____

	J	F	M	A	M	J	J	A	S	O	N	D
SOW:												
PLANT OUT:												
HARVEST/BLOOM:												

SOWING METHOD:
Indoors / Direct / Seed bed

NEEDS SUPPORT: Yes / No

FINAL GROWING LOCATION:
Outdoors / Polytunnel / Greenhouse

FEED WITH: _____
Frequency: _____

PLANT SPACING: _____

SOW IN SUCCESSION: Yes / No
Frequency: _____

SOIL TYPE: _____

MULCH: Yes/No MANURE: Yes/No
Type: _____ Type: _____

SUN: All day / Partial / Shade

ATTRACTOR FOR: _____
_____

WATER FREQUENCY:
_____

REPELLENT TO: _____
_____

FROST TOLERANCE: Yes / No

PEST ISSUES: SOLUTIONS:
_____   _____
_____   _____
_____   _____

CROP ROTATION FREQUENCY:
_____

OTHER THINGS TO NOTE: _____
_____

PLANT INFORMATION SHEET

PLANT NAME: _____

VARIETY: _____

TYPE: Seed / Cutting / Plug Plant / Bulb

LIFE CYCLE: Annual / Biennial / Perennial

GOOD COMPANION FOR:
_____
_____
_____

BAD COMPANION FOR:
_____
_____
_____

	J	F	M	A	M	J	J	A	S	O	N	D
SOW:												
PLANT OUT:												
HARVEST/BLOOM:												

SOWING METHOD: Indoors / Direct / Seed bed

FINAL GROWING LOCATION: Outdoors / Polytunnel / Greenhouse

PLANT SPACING: _____

SOIL TYPE: _____

SUN: All day / Partial / Shade

ATTRACTOR FOR: _____
_____

REPELLENT TO: _____
_____

CROP ROTATION FREQUENCY:
_____

NEEDS SUPPORT: Yes / No

FEED WITH: _____
Frequency: _____

SOW IN SUCCESSION: Yes / No
Frequency: _____

MULCH: Yes/No   MANURE: Yes/No
Type: _____   Type: _____

WATER FREQUENCY:
_____

FROST TOLERANCE: Yes / No

PEST ISSUES: SOLUTIONS:
_____   _____
_____   _____

OTHER THINGS TO NOTE: _____
_____

PLANT INFORMATION SHEET

PLANT NAME: _____

VARIETY: _____

TYPE:
Seed / Cutting / Plug Plant / Bulb

LIFE CYCLE:
Annual / Biennial / Perennial

GOOD COMPANION FOR:
_____
_____
_____

BAD COMPANION FOR:
_____
_____
_____

	J	F	M	A	M	J	J	A	S	O	N	D
SOW:												
PLANT OUT:												
HARVEST/BLOOM:												

SOWING METHOD:
Indoors / Direct / Seed bed

FINAL GROWING LOCATION:
Outdoors / Polytunnel / Greenhouse

PLANT SPACING: _____

SOIL TYPE: _____

SUN: All day / Partial / Shade

ATTRACTOR FOR: _____
_____

REPELLENT TO: _____
_____

CROP ROTATION FREQUENCY:
_____

NEEDS SUPPORT: Yes / No

FEED WITH: _____
Frequency: _____

SOW IN SUCCESSION: Yes / No
Frequency: _____

MULCH: Yes/No
Type: _____

MANURE: Yes/No
Type: _____

WATER FREQUENCY:
_____

FROST TOLERANCE: Yes / No

PEST ISSUES:
_____
_____

SOLUTIONS:
_____
_____

OTHER THINGS TO NOTE: _____
_____

PLANT INFORMATION SHEET

PLANT NAME: _____ VARIETY: _____

TYPE: Seed / Cutting / Plug Plant / Bulb

LIFE CYCLE: Annual / Biennial / Perennial

GOOD COMPANION FOR:
_____
_____
_____

BAD COMPANION FOR:
_____
_____
_____

	J	F	M	A	M	J	J	A	S	O	N	D
SOW:												
PLANT OUT:												
HARVEST/BLOOM:												

SOWING METHOD: Indoors / Direct / Seed bed

FINAL GROWING LOCATION: Outdoors / Polytunnel / Greenhouse

PLANT SPACING: _____

SOIL TYPE: _____

SUN: All day / Partial / Shade

ATTRACTOR FOR: _____
_____

REPELLENT TO: _____
_____

CROP ROTATION FREQUENCY: _____

NEEDS SUPPORT: Yes / No

FEED WITH: _____
Frequency: _____

SOW IN SUCCESSION: Yes / No
Frequency: _____

MULCH: Yes/No   MANURE: Yes/No
Type: _____   Type: _____

WATER FREQUENCY: _____

FROST TOLERANCE: Yes / No

PEST ISSUES: SOLUTIONS:
_____   _____
_____   _____
_____   _____

OTHER THINGS TO NOTE: _____
_____

PLANT INFORMATION SHEET

PLANT NAME: _____

VARIETY: _____

TYPE:
Seed / Cutting / Plug Plant / Bulb

LIFE CYCLE:
Annual / Biennial / Perennial

GOOD COMPANION FOR:
_____
_____
_____

BAD COMPANION FOR:
_____
_____
_____

	J	F	M	A	M	J	J	A	S	O	N	D
SOW:												
PLANT OUT:												
HARVEST/BLOOM:												

SOWING METHOD:
Indoors / Direct / Seed bed

FINAL GROWING LOCATION:
Outdoors / Polytunnel / Greenhouse

PLANT SPACING: _____

SOIL TYPE: _____

SUN: All day / Partial / Shade

ATTRACTOR FOR: _____
_____

REPELLENT TO: _____
_____

CROP ROTATION FREQUENCY:
_____

NEEDS SUPPORT: Yes / No

FEED WITH: _____
Frequency: _____

SOW IN SUCCESSION: Yes / No
Frequency: _____

MULCH: Yes/No   MANURE: Yes/No
Type: _____   Type: _____

WATER FREQUENCY:
_____

FROST TOLERANCE: Yes / No

PEST ISSUES: SOLUTIONS:
_____   _____
_____   _____
_____   _____

OTHER THINGS TO NOTE: _____
_____

PLANT INFORMATION SHEET

PLANT NAME: _____

VARIETY: _____

TYPE:
Seed / Cutting / Plug Plant / Bulb

LIFE CYCLE:
Annual / Biennial / Perennial

GOOD COMPANION FOR:
_____
_____

BAD COMPANION FOR:
_____
_____

	J	F	M	A	M	J	J	A	S	O	N	D
SOW:												
PLANT OUT:												
HARVEST/BLOOM:												

SOWING METHOD:
Indoors / Direct / Seed bed

NEEDS SUPPORT: Yes / No

FINAL GROWING LOCATION:
Outdoors / Polytunnel / Greenhouse

FEED WITH: _____
Frequency: _____

PLANT SPACING: _____

SOW IN SUCCESSION: Yes / No
Frequency: _____

SOIL TYPE: _____

MULCH: Yes/No   MANURE: Yes/No
Type: _____   Type: _____

SUN: All day / Partial / Shade

ATTRACTOR FOR: _____
_____

WATER FREQUENCY:
_____

REPELLENT TO: _____
_____

FROST TOLERANCE: Yes / No

PEST ISSUES: SOLUTIONS:
_____   _____
_____   _____

CROP ROTATION FREQUENCY:
_____

OTHER THINGS TO NOTE: _____
_____

PLANT INFORMATION SHEET

PLANT NAME: _____ VARIETY: _____

TYPE:
Seed / Cutting / Plug Plant / Bulb

LIFE CYCLE:
Annual / Biennial / Perennial

GOOD COMPANION FOR:
_____
_____
_____

BAD COMPANION FOR:
_____
_____
_____

	J	F	M	A	M	J	J	A	S	O	N	D
SOW:												
PLANT OUT:												
HARVEST/BLOOM:												

SOWING METHOD:
Indoors / Direct / Seed bed

FINAL GROWING LOCATION:
Outdoors / Polytunnel / Greenhouse

PLANT SPACING: _____

SOIL TYPE: _____

SUN: All day / Partial / Shade

ATTRACTOR FOR: _____
_____

REPELLENT TO: _____
_____

CROP ROTATION FREQUENCY:
_____

NEEDS SUPPORT: Yes / No

FEED WITH: _____
Frequency: _____

SOW IN SUCCESSION: Yes / No
Frequency: _____

MULCH: Yes/No   MANURE: Yes/No
Type: _____   Type: _____

WATER FREQUENCY:
_____

FROST TOLERANCE: Yes / No

PEST ISSUES: SOLUTIONS:
_____   _____
_____   _____
_____   _____

OTHER THINGS TO NOTE: _____
_____

PLANT INFORMATION SHEET

PLANT NAME: _____

VARIETY: _____

TYPE:
Seed / Cutting / Plug Plant / Bulb

LIFE CYCLE:
Annual / Biennial / Perennial

GOOD COMPANION FOR:
_____
_____
_____

BAD COMPANION FOR:
_____
_____
_____

	J	F	M	A	M	J	J	A	S	O	N	D
SOW:												
PLANT OUT:												
HARVEST/BLOOM:												

SOWING METHOD:
Indoors / Direct / Seed bed

NEEDS SUPPORT: Yes / No

FINAL GROWING LOCATION:
Outdoors / Polytunnel / Greenhouse

FEED WITH: _____
Frequency: _____

PLANT SPACING: _____

SOW IN SUCCESSION: Yes / No
Frequency: _____

SOIL TYPE: _____

MULCH: Yes/No   MANURE: Yes/No
Type: _____   Type: _____

SUN: All day / Partial / Shade

ATTRACTOR FOR: _____
_____

WATER FREQUENCY:
_____

REPELLENT TO: _____
_____

FROST TOLERANCE: Yes / No

PEST ISSUES: SOLUTIONS:
_____   _____
_____   _____
_____   _____

CROP ROTATION FREQUENCY:
_____

OTHER THINGS TO NOTE: _____
_____

PLANT INFORMATION SHEET

PLANT NAME: _____

VARIETY: _____

TYPE:
Seed / Cutting / Plug Plant / Bulb

LIFE CYCLE:
Annual / Biennial / Perennial

GOOD COMPANION FOR:
_____
_____
_____

BAD COMPANION FOR:
_____
_____
_____

	J	F	M	A	M	J	J	A	S	O	N	D
SOW:												
PLANT OUT:												
HARVEST/BLOOM:												

SOWING METHOD:
Indoors / Direct / Seed bed

FINAL GROWING LOCATION:
Outdoors / Polytunnel / Greenhouse

PLANT SPACING: _____

SOIL TYPE: _____

SUN: All day / Partial / Shade

ATTRACTOR FOR: _____
_____

REPELLENT TO: _____
_____

CROP ROTATION FREQUENCY:
_____

NEEDS SUPPORT: Yes / No

FEED WITH: _____
Frequency: _____

SOW IN SUCCESSION: Yes / No
Frequency: _____

MULCH: Yes/No   MANURE: Yes/No
Type: _____   Type: _____

WATER FREQUENCY:
_____

FROST TOLERANCE: Yes / No

PEST ISSUES: SOLUTIONS:
_____   _____
_____   _____
_____   _____

OTHER THINGS TO NOTE: _____
_____

PLANT INFORMATION SHEET

PLANT NAME: _____

VARIETY: _____

TYPE:
Seed / Cutting / Plug Plant / Bulb

LIFE CYCLE:
Annual / Biennial / Perennial

GOOD COMPANION FOR:
_____
_____
_____

BAD COMPANION FOR:
_____
_____
_____

	J	F	M	A	M	J	J	A	S	O	N	D
SOW:												
PLANT OUT:												
HARVEST/BLOOM:												

SOWING METHOD:
Indoors / Direct / Seed bed

FINAL GROWING LOCATION:
Outdoors / Polytunnel / Greenhouse

PLANT SPACING: _____

SOIL TYPE: _____

SUN: All day / Partial / Shade

ATTRACTOR FOR: _____
_____

REPELLENT TO: _____
_____

CROP ROTATION FREQUENCY:
_____

NEEDS SUPPORT: Yes / No

FEED WITH: _____
Frequency: _____

SOW IN SUCCESSION: Yes / No
Frequency: _____

MULCH: Yes/No   MANURE: Yes/No
Type: _____   Type: _____

WATER FREQUENCY:
_____

FROST TOLERANCE: Yes / No

PEST ISSUES: SOLUTIONS:
_____   _____
_____   _____

OTHER THINGS TO NOTE: _____
_____

PLANT INFORMATION SHEET

PLANT NAME: _____

VARIETY: _____

TYPE:
Seed / Cutting / Plug Plant / Bulb

LIFE CYCLE:
Annual / Biennial / Perennial

GOOD COMPANION FOR:
_____
_____
_____

BAD COMPANION FOR:
_____
_____
_____

	J	F	M	A	M	J	J	A	S	O	N	D
SOW:												
PLANT OUT:												
HARVEST/BLOOM:												

SOWING METHOD:
Indoors / Direct / Seed bed

FINAL GROWING LOCATION:
Outdoors / Polytunnel / Greenhouse

PLANT SPACING: _____

SOIL TYPE: _____

SUN: All day / Partial / Shade

ATTRACTOR FOR: _____
_____

REPELLENT TO: _____
_____

CROP ROTATION FREQUENCY:
_____

NEEDS SUPPORT: Yes / No

FEED WITH: _____
Frequency: _____

SOW IN SUCCESSION: Yes / No
Frequency: _____

MULCH: Yes/No   MANURE: Yes/No
Type: _____   Type: _____

WATER FREQUENCY:
_____

FROST TOLERANCE: Yes / No

PEST ISSUES: SOLUTIONS:
_____   _____
_____   _____
_____   _____

OTHER THINGS TO NOTE: _____
_____

PLANT INFORMATION SHEET

PLANT NAME: _____

VARIETY: _____

TYPE:
Seed / Cutting / Plug Plant / Bulb

LIFE CYCLE:
Annual / Biennial / Perennial

GOOD COMPANION FOR:
_____
_____
_____

BAD COMPANION FOR:
_____
_____
_____

	J	F	M	A	M	J	J	A	S	O	N	D
SOW:												
PLANT OUT:												
HARVEST/BLOOM:												

SOWING METHOD:
Indoors / Direct / Seed bed

NEEDS SUPPORT: Yes / No

FINAL GROWING LOCATION:
Outdoors / Polytunnel / Greenhouse

FEED WITH: _____
Frequency: _____

PLANT SPACING: _____

SOW IN SUCCESSION: Yes / No
Frequency: _____

SOIL TYPE: _____

MULCH: Yes/No   MANURE: Yes/No
Type: _____   Type: _____

SUN: All day / Partial / Shade

ATTRACTOR FOR: _____
_____

WATER FREQUENCY:
_____

REPELLENT TO: _____
_____

FROST TOLERANCE: Yes / No

PEST ISSUES: SOLUTIONS:
_____   _____
_____   _____

CROP ROTATION FREQUENCY:
_____

OTHER THINGS TO NOTE: _____
_____

PLANT INFORMATION SHEET

PLANT NAME:_____   VARIETY:_____

TYPE:
Seed / Cutting / Plug Plant / Bulb

LIFE CYCLE:
Annual / Biennial / Perennial

GOOD COMPANION FOR:
_____
_____
_____

BAD COMPANION FOR:
_____
_____
_____

	J	F	M	A	M	J	J	A	S	O	N	D
SOW:												
PLANT OUT:												
HARVEST/BLOOM:												

SOWING METHOD:
Indoors / Direct / Seed bed

FINAL GROWING LOCATION:
Outdoors / Polytunnel / Greenhouse

PLANT SPACING:_____

SOIL TYPE: _____

SUN: All day / Partial / Shade

ATTRACTOR FOR: _____
_____

REPELLENT TO: _____
_____

CROP ROTATION FREQUENCY:
_____

NEEDS SUPPORT: Yes / No

FEED WITH: _____
Frequency: _____

SOW IN SUCCESSION: Yes / No
Frequency: _____

MULCH: Yes/No   MANURE: Yes/No
Type: _____   Type: _____

WATER FREQUENCY:
_____

FROST TOLERANCE: Yes / No

PEST ISSUES: SOLUTIONS:
_____   _____
_____   _____

OTHER THINGS TO NOTE: _____
_____

PLANT INFORMATION SHEET

PLANT NAME: _____

VARIETY: _____

TYPE:
Seed / Cutting / Plug Plant / Bulb

LIFE CYCLE:
Annual / Biennial / Perennial

GOOD COMPANION FOR:
_____
_____

BAD COMPANION FOR:
_____
_____

	J	F	M	A	M	J	J	A	S	O	N	D
SOW:												
PLANT OUT:												
HARVEST/BLOOM:												

SOWING METHOD:
Indoors / Direct / Seed bed

NEEDS SUPPORT: Yes / No

FINAL GROWING LOCATION:
Outdoors / Polytunnel / Greenhouse

FEED WITH: _____
Frequency: _____

PLANT SPACING: _____

SOW IN SUCCESSION: Yes / No
Frequency: _____

SOIL TYPE: _____

MULCH: Yes/No   MANURE: Yes/No
Type: _____   Type: _____

SUN: All day / Partial / Shade

ATTRACTOR FOR: _____
_____

WATER FREQUENCY:
_____

REPELLENT TO: _____
_____

FROST TOLERANCE: Yes / No

PEST ISSUES: SOLUTIONS:
_____   _____
_____   _____

CROP ROTATION FREQUENCY:
_____

OTHER THINGS TO NOTE: _____
_____

PLANT INFORMATION SHEET

PLANT NAME: _____ VARIETY: _____

TYPE:
Seed / Cutting / Plug Plant / Bulb

LIFE CYCLE:
Annual / Biennial / Perennial

GOOD COMPANION FOR:
_____
_____
_____

BAD COMPANION FOR:
_____
_____
_____

	J	F	M	A	M	J	J	A	S	O	N	D
SOW:												
PLANT OUT:												
HARVEST/BLOOM:												

SOWING METHOD:
Indoors / Direct / Seed bed

FINAL GROWING LOCATION:
Outdoors / Polytunnel / Greenhouse

PLANT SPACING: _____

SOIL TYPE: _____

SUN: All day / Partial / Shade

ATTRACTOR FOR: _____
_____

REPELLENT TO: _____
_____

CROP ROTATION FREQUENCY:
_____

NEEDS SUPPORT: Yes / No

FEED WITH: _____
Frequency: _____

SOW IN SUCCESSION: Yes / No
Frequency: _____

MULCH: Yes/No   MANURE: Yes/No
Type: _____   Type: _____

WATER FREQUENCY:
_____

FROST TOLERANCE: Yes / No

PEST ISSUES: SOLUTIONS:
_____   _____
_____   _____
_____   _____

OTHER THINGS TO NOTE: _____
_____

PLANT INFORMATION SHEET

PLANT NAME: _____

VARIETY: _____

TYPE:
Seed / Cutting / Plug Plant / Bulb

LIFE CYCLE:
Annual / Biennial / Perennial

GOOD COMPANION FOR:
_____
_____
_____

BAD COMPANION FOR:
_____
_____
_____

	J	F	M	A	M	J	J	A	S	O	N	D
SOW:												
PLANT OUT:												
HARVEST/BLOOM:												

SOWING METHOD:
Indoors / Direct / Seed bed

NEEDS SUPPORT: Yes / No

FEED WITH: _____
Frequency: _____

FINAL GROWING LOCATION:
Outdoors / Polytunnel / Greenhouse

SOW IN SUCCESSION: Yes / No
Frequency: _____

PLANT SPACING: _____

MULCH: Yes/No   MANURE: Yes/No
Type: _____   Type: _____

SOIL TYPE: _____

SUN: All day / Partial / Shade

ATTRACTOR FOR: _____
_____

WATER FREQUENCY:
_____

FROST TOLERANCE: Yes / No

REPELLENT TO: _____
_____

PEST ISSUES: SOLUTIONS:
_____   _____
_____   _____

CROP ROTATION FREQUENCY:
_____

OTHER THINGS TO NOTE: _____
_____

PLANT INFORMATION SHEET

PLANT NAME: _____

VARIETY: _____

TYPE:
Seed / Cutting / Plug Plant / Bulb

LIFE CYCLE:
Annual / Biennial / Perennial

GOOD COMPANION FOR:
_____
_____
_____

BAD COMPANION FOR:
_____
_____
_____

	J	F	M	A	M	J	J	A	S	O	N	D
SOW:												
PLANT OUT:												
HARVEST/BLOOM:												

SOWING METHOD:
Indoors / Direct / Seed bed

FINAL GROWING LOCATION:
Outdoors / Polytunnel / Greenhouse

PLANT SPACING: _____

SOIL TYPE: _____

SUN: All day / Partial / Shade

ATTRACTOR FOR: _____
_____

REPELLENT TO: _____
_____

CROP ROTATION FREQUENCY:
_____

NEEDS SUPPORT: Yes / No

FEED WITH: _____
Frequency: _____

SOW IN SUCCESSION: Yes / No
Frequency: _____

MULCH: Yes/No   MANURE: Yes/No
Type: _____   Type: _____

WATER FREQUENCY:
_____

FROST TOLERANCE: Yes / No

PEST ISSUES: SOLUTIONS:
_____   _____
_____   _____

OTHER THINGS TO NOTE: _____
_____

PLANT INFORMATION SHEET

PLANT NAME: _____   VARIETY: _____

TYPE: Seed / Cutting / Plug Plant / Bulb

LIFE CYCLE: Annual / Biennial / Perennial

GOOD COMPANION FOR:
_____
_____
_____

BAD COMPANION FOR:
_____
_____
_____

	J	F	M	A	M	J	J	A	S	O	N	D
SOW:												
PLANT OUT:												
HARVEST/BLOOM:												

SOWING METHOD: Indoors / Direct / Seed bed

FINAL GROWING LOCATION: Outdoors / Polytunnel / Greenhouse

PLANT SPACING: _____

SOIL TYPE: _____

SUN: All day / Partial / Shade

ATTRACTOR FOR: _____
_____

REPELLENT TO: _____
_____

CROP ROTATION FREQUENCY: _____

NEEDS SUPPORT: Yes / No

FEED WITH: _____
Frequency: _____

SOW IN SUCCESSION: Yes / No
Frequency: _____

MULCH: Yes/No   MANURE: Yes/No
Type: _____   Type: _____

WATER FREQUENCY: _____

FROST TOLERANCE: Yes / No

PEST ISSUES: SOLUTIONS:
_____   _____
_____   _____

OTHER THINGS TO NOTE: _____
_____

PLANT INFORMATION SHEET

PLANT NAME: _____

VARIETY: _____

TYPE:
Seed / Cutting / Plug Plant / Bulb

LIFE CYCLE:
Annual / Biennial / Perennial

GOOD COMPANION FOR:
_____
_____
_____

BAD COMPANION FOR:
_____
_____
_____

	J	F	M	A	M	J	J	A	S	O	N	D
SOW:												
PLANT OUT:												
HARVEST/BLOOM:												

SOWING METHOD:
Indoors / Direct / Seed bed

FINAL GROWING LOCATION:
Outdoors / Polytunnel / Greenhouse

PLANT SPACING: _____

SOIL TYPE: _____

SUN: All day / Partial / Shade

ATTRACTOR FOR: _____
_____

REPELLENT TO: _____
_____

CROP ROTATION FREQUENCY:
_____

NEEDS SUPPORT: Yes / No

FEED WITH: _____
Frequency: _____

SOW IN SUCCESSION: Yes / No
Frequency: _____

MULCH: Yes/No   MANURE: Yes/No
Type: _____   Type: _____

WATER FREQUENCY:
_____

FROST TOLERANCE: Yes / No

PEST ISSUES: SOLUTIONS:
_____   _____
_____   _____
_____   _____

OTHER THINGS TO NOTE: _____
_____

PLANT INFORMATION SHEET

PLANT NAME: _____ VARIETY: _____

TYPE: Seed / Cutting / Plug Plant / Bulb

LIFE CYCLE: Annual / Biennial / Perennial

GOOD COMPANION FOR:
_____
_____
_____

BAD COMPANION FOR:
_____
_____
_____

	J	F	M	A	M	J	J	A	S	O	N	D
SOW:												
PLANT OUT:												
HARVEST/BLOOM:												

SOWING METHOD: Indoors / Direct / Seed bed

FINAL GROWING LOCATION: Outdoors / Polytunnel / Greenhouse

PLANT SPACING: _____

SOIL TYPE: _____

SUN: All day / Partial / Shade

ATTRACTOR FOR: _____
_____

REPELLENT TO: _____
_____

CROP ROTATION FREQUENCY: _____
_____

NEEDS SUPPORT: Yes / No

FEED WITH: _____
Frequency: _____

SOW IN SUCCESSION: Yes / No
Frequency: _____

MULCH: Yes/No   MANURE: Yes/No
Type: _____   Type: _____

WATER FREQUENCY: _____

FROST TOLERANCE: Yes / No

PEST ISSUES: _____   SOLUTIONS: _____
_____   _____

OTHER THINGS TO NOTE: _____
_____

PLANT INFORMATION SHEET

PLANT NAME: _____

VARIETY: _____

TYPE:
Seed / Cutting / Plug Plant / Bulb

LIFE CYCLE:
Annual / Biennial / Perennial

GOOD COMPANION FOR:
_____
_____
_____

BAD COMPANION FOR:
_____
_____
_____

	J	F	M	A	M	J	J	A	S	O	N	D
SOW:												
PLANT OUT:												
HARVEST/BLOOM:												

SOWING METHOD:
Indoors / Direct / Seed bed

FINAL GROWING LOCATION:
Outdoors / Polytunnel / Greenhouse

PLANT SPACING: _____

SOIL TYPE: _____

SUN: All day / Partial / Shade

ATTRACTOR FOR: _____
_____

REPELLENT TO: _____
_____

CROP ROTATION FREQUENCY:
_____

NEEDS SUPPORT: Yes / No

FEED WITH: _____
Frequency: _____

SOW IN SUCCESSION: Yes / No
Frequency: _____

MULCH: Yes/No   MANURE: Yes/No
Type: _____   Type: _____

WATER FREQUENCY:
_____

FROST TOLERANCE: Yes / No

PEST ISSUES: SOLUTIONS:
_____   _____
_____   _____
_____   _____

OTHER THINGS TO NOTE: _____
_____

PLANT INFORMATION SHEET

PLANT NAME: _____

VARIETY: _____

TYPE:
Seed / Cutting / Plug Plant / Bulb

LIFE CYCLE:
Annual / Biennial / Perennial

GOOD COMPANION FOR:
_____
_____
_____

BAD COMPANION FOR:
_____
_____
_____

	J	F	M	A	M	J	J	A	S	O	N	D
SOW:												
PLANT OUT:												
HARVEST/BLOOM:												

SOWING METHOD:
Indoors / Direct / Seed bed

FINAL GROWING LOCATION:
Outdoors / Polytunnel / Greenhouse

PLANT SPACING: _____

SOIL TYPE: _____

SUN: All day / Partial / Shade

ATTRACTOR FOR: _____
_____

REPELLENT TO: _____
_____

CROP ROTATION FREQUENCY:
_____

NEEDS SUPPORT: Yes / No

FEED WITH: _____
Frequency: _____

SOW IN SUCCESSION: Yes / No
Frequency: _____

MULCH: Yes/No   MANURE: Yes/No
Type: _____   Type: _____

WATER FREQUENCY:
_____

FROST TOLERANCE: Yes / No

PEST ISSUES: SOLUTIONS:
_____   _____
_____   _____

OTHER THINGS TO NOTE: _____
_____

PLANT INFORMATION SHEET

PLANT NAME: _____   VARIETY: _____

TYPE:
Seed / Cutting / Plug Plant / Bulb

LIFE CYCLE:
Annual / Biennial / Perennial

GOOD COMPANION FOR:
_____
_____
_____

BAD COMPANION FOR:
_____
_____
_____

	J	F	M	A	M	J	J	A	S	O	N	D
SOW:												
PLANT OUT:												
HARVEST/BLOOM:												

SOWING METHOD:
Indoors / Direct / Seed bed

NEEDS SUPPORT: Yes / No

FINAL GROWING LOCATION:
Outdoors / Polytunnel / Greenhouse

FEED WITH: _____
Frequency: _____

PLANT SPACING: _____

SOW IN SUCCESSION: Yes / No
Frequency: _____

SOIL TYPE: _____

MULCH: Yes/No   MANURE: Yes/No
Type: _____   Type: _____

SUN: All day / Partial / Shade

ATTRACTOR FOR: _____
_____

WATER FREQUENCY:
_____

REPELLENT TO: _____
_____

FROST TOLERANCE: Yes / No

PEST ISSUES: SOLUTIONS:
_____   _____
_____   _____

CROP ROTATION FREQUENCY:
_____

OTHER THINGS TO NOTE: _____
_____

PLANT INFORMATION SHEET

PLANT NAME: _____ VARIETY: _____

TYPE:
Seed / Cutting / Plug Plant / Bulb

LIFE CYCLE:
Annual / Biennial / Perennial

GOOD COMPANION FOR:
_____
_____
_____

BAD COMPANION FOR:
_____
_____
_____

	J	F	M	A	M	J	J	A	S	O	N	D
SOW:												
PLANT OUT:												
HARVEST/BLOOM:												

SOWING METHOD:
Indoors / Direct / Seed bed

FINAL GROWING LOCATION:
Outdoors / Polytunnel / Greenhouse

PLANT SPACING: _____

SOIL TYPE: _____

SUN: All day / Partial / Shade

ATTRACTOR FOR: _____
_____

REPELLENT TO: _____
_____

CROP ROTATION FREQUENCY:
_____

NEEDS SUPPORT: Yes / No

FEED WITH: _____
Frequency: _____

SOW IN SUCCESSION: Yes / No
Frequency: _____

MULCH: Yes/No   MANURE: Yes/No
Type: _____   Type: _____

WATER FREQUENCY:
_____

FROST TOLERANCE: Yes / No

PEST ISSUES:
_____
_____
_____

SOLUTIONS:
_____
_____
_____

OTHER THINGS TO NOTE: _____
_____

PLANT INFORMATION SHEET

PLANT NAME: _____

VARIETY: _____

TYPE:
Seed / Cutting / Plug Plant / Bulb

LIFE CYCLE:
Annual / Biennial / Perennial

GOOD COMPANION FOR:
_____
_____
_____

BAD COMPANION FOR:
_____
_____
_____

	J	F	M	A	M	J	J	A	S	O	N	D
SOW:												
PLANT OUT:												
HARVEST/BLOOM:												

SOWING METHOD:
Indoors / Direct / Seed bed

FINAL GROWING LOCATION:
Outdoors / Polytunnel / Greenhouse

PLANT SPACING: _____

SOIL TYPE: _____

SUN: All day / Partial / Shade

ATTRACTOR FOR: _____
_____

REPELLENT TO: _____
_____

CROP ROTATION FREQUENCY:
_____

NEEDS SUPPORT: Yes / No

FEED WITH: _____
Frequency: _____

SOW IN SUCCESSION: Yes / No
Frequency: _____

MULCH: Yes/No   MANURE: Yes/No
Type: _____   Type: _____

WATER FREQUENCY:
_____

FROST TOLERANCE: Yes / No

PEST ISSUES: SOLUTIONS:
_____ _____
_____ _____
_____ _____

OTHER THINGS TO NOTE: _____
_____

PLANT INFORMATION SHEET

PLANT NAME: _____

VARIETY: _____

TYPE:
Seed / Cutting / Plug Plant / Bulb

LIFE CYCLE:
Annual / Biennial / Perennial

GOOD COMPANION FOR:
_____
_____
_____

BAD COMPANION FOR:
_____
_____
_____

	J	F	M	A	M	J	J	A	S	O	N	D
SOW:												
PLANT OUT:												
HARVEST/BLOOM:												

SOWING METHOD:
Indoors / Direct / Seed bed

NEEDS SUPPORT: Yes / No

FEED WITH: _____
Frequency: _____

FINAL GROWING LOCATION:
Outdoors / Polytunnel / Greenhouse

SOW IN SUCCESSION: Yes / No
Frequency: _____

PLANT SPACING: _____

SOIL TYPE: _____

MULCH: Yes/No   MANURE: Yes/No
Type: _____   Type: _____

SUN: All day / Partial / Shade

ATTRACTOR FOR: _____
_____

WATER FREQUENCY:
_____

REPELLENT TO: _____
_____

FROST TOLERANCE: Yes / No

PEST ISSUES: SOLUTIONS:
_____   _____
_____   _____
_____   _____

CROP ROTATION FREQUENCY:
_____

OTHER THINGS TO NOTE: _____
_____

PLANT INFORMATION SHEET

PLANT NAME: _____

VARIETY: _____

TYPE:
Seed / Cutting / Plug Plant / Bulb

LIFE CYCLE:
Annual / Biennial / Perennial

GOOD COMPANION FOR:
_____
_____
_____

BAD COMPANION FOR:
_____
_____
_____

	J	F	M	A	M	J	J	A	S	O	N	D
SOW:												
PLANT OUT:												
HARVEST/BLOOM:												

SOWING METHOD:
Indoors / Direct / Seed bed

NEEDS SUPPORT: Yes / No

FINAL GROWING LOCATION:
Outdoors / Polytunnel / Greenhouse

FEED WITH: _____
Frequency: _____

PLANT SPACING: _____

SOW IN SUCCESSION: Yes / No
Frequency: _____

SOIL TYPE: _____

MULCH: Yes/No   MANURE: Yes/No
Type: _____   Type: _____

SUN: All day / Partial / Shade

ATTRACTOR FOR: _____
_____

WATER FREQUENCY:
_____

REPELLENT TO: _____
_____

FROST TOLERANCE: Yes / No

PEST ISSUES: SOLUTIONS:
_____   _____
_____   _____

CROP ROTATION FREQUENCY:
_____

OTHER THINGS TO NOTE: _____
_____

PLANT INFORMATION SHEET

PLANT NAME: _____

VARIETY: _____

TYPE:
Seed / Cutting / Plug Plant / Bulb

LIFE CYCLE:
Annual / Biennial / Perennial

GOOD COMPANION FOR:
_____
_____
_____

BAD COMPANION FOR:
_____
_____
_____

	J	F	M	A	M	J	J	A	S	O	N	D
SOW:												
PLANT OUT:												
HARVEST/BLOOM:												

SOWING METHOD:
Indoors / Direct / Seed bed

NEEDS SUPPORT: Yes / No

FINAL GROWING LOCATION:
Outdoors / Polytunnel / Greenhouse

FEED WITH: _____
Frequency: _____

PLANT SPACING: _____

SOW IN SUCCESSION: Yes / No
Frequency: _____

SOIL TYPE: _____

MULCH: Yes/No   MANURE: Yes/No
Type: _____   Type: _____

SUN: All day / Partial / Shade

ATTRACTOR FOR: _____
_____

WATER FREQUENCY:
_____

REPELLENT TO: _____
_____

FROST TOLERANCE: Yes / No

PEST ISSUES: SOLUTIONS:
_____   _____
_____   _____
_____   _____

CROP ROTATION FREQUENCY:
_____

OTHER THINGS TO NOTE: _____
_____

Printed in Great Britain
by Amazon